Peacock Pie

By the same author

COLLECTED RHYMES AND VERSES
STORIES FROM THE BIBLE
TALES TOLD AGAIN (Faber Fanfares)

Peacock Pie

a book of rhymes

by

WALTER DE LA MARE

with drawings by

EDWARD ARDIZZONE

FABER
FANFARES

First published in Faber Paperbacks 1958
by Faber and Faber Limited
3 Queen Square, London WC1
Reprinted 1963, 1967, 1970 and 1974
First published in Fanfares edition 1980
Printed in Great Britain by
Jarrold and Sons Ltd, Norwich
All rights reserved

British Library Cataloguing in Publication Data

De la Mare, Walter
Peacock pie. – (Faber fanfares).
I. Title II. Ardizzone, Edward
821'.9'12   PZ8.3

ISBN 0–571–18014–0

Contents

The Horseman

I heard a horseman
  Ride over the hill;
The moon shone clear,
The night was still;
His helm was silver,
  And pale was he;
And the horse he rode
  Was of ivory.

Alas, Alack!

Ann, Ann!
  Come! quick as you can!
There's a fish that *talks*
  In the frying-pan.
Out of the fat,
  As clear as glass,
He put up his mouth
  And moaned 'Alas!'
Oh, most mournful,
  'Alas, alack!'
Then turned to his sizzling,
  And sank him back.

Tired Tim

Poor tired Tim! It's sad for him.
He lags the long bright morning through,
Ever so tired of nothing to do;
He moons and mopes the livelong day,
Nothing to think about, nothing to say;
Up to bed with his candle to creep,
Too tired to yawn, too tired to sleep:
Poor tired Tim! It's sad for him.

13

Mima

Jemima is my name,
  But oh, I have another;
My father always calls me Meg,
  And so do Bob and mother;
Only my sister, jealous of
  The strands of my bright hair,
'Jemima—Mima—Mima!'
  Calls, mocking, up the stair.

The Huntsmen

Three jolly gentlemen,
  In coats of red,
Rode their horses
  Up to bed.

Three jolly gentlemen
  Snored till morn,
Their horses champing
  The golden corn.

Three jolly gentlemen,
  At break of day,
Came clitter-clatter down the stairs
And galloped away.

The Bandog

Has anybody seen my Mopser?——
  A comely dog is he,
With hair of the colour of a Charles the Fifth,
  And teeth like ships at sea,
His tail it curls straight upwards,
  His ears stand two abreast,
And he answers to the simple name of Mopser,
  When civilly addressed.

I Can't Abear

I can't abear a Butcher,
   I can't abide his meat,
The ugliest shop of all is his,
   The ugliest in the street;
Bakers' are warm, cobblers' dark,
   Chemists' burn watery lights;
But oh, the sawdust butcher's shop,
   That ugliest of sights!

The Dunce

Why does he still keep ticking?
  Why does his round white face
Stare at me over the books and ink,
  And mock at my disgrace?
Why does that thrush call, 'Dunce, dunce, dunce!'?
  Why does that bluebottle buzz?
Why does the sun so silent shine?—
  And what do I care if it does?

Chicken

Clapping her platter stood plump Bess,
  And all across the green
Came scampering in, on wing and claw,
  Chicken fat and lean:—
Dorking, Spaniard, Cochin China,
  Bantams sleek and small,
Like feathers blown in a great wind,
  They came at Bessie's call.

Some One

Some one came knocking
　At my wee, small door;
Some one came knocking,
　I'm sure—sure—sure;

I listened, I opened,
  I looked to left and right,
But naught there was a-stirring
  In the still dark night;
Only the busy beetle
  Tap-tapping in the wall,
Only from the forest
  The screech-owl's call,
Only the cricket whistling
  While the dewdrops fall,
So I know not who came knocking,
  At all, at all, at all.

Bread and Cherries

'Cherries, ripe cherries!'
  The old woman cried,
In her snowy white apron,
  And basket beside;
And the little boys came,
  Eyes shining, cheeks red,
To buy a bag of cherries,
To eat with their bread.

Old Shellover

'Come!' said Old Shellover.
'What?' says Creep.
'The horny old Gardener's fast asleep;
The fat cock Thrush
To his nest has gone;
And the dew shines bright
In the rising Moon;
Old Sallie Worm from her hole doth peep:
Come!' said Old Shellover.
'Ay!' said Creep.

Hapless

Hapless, hapless, I must be
All the hours of life I see,
Since my foolish nurse did once
Bed me on her leggen bones;
Since my mother did not weel
To snip my nails with blades of steel.
Had they laid me on a pillow
In a cot of water willow,
Had they bitten finger and thumb,
Not to such ill hap I had come.

The Little Bird

My dear Daddie bought a mansion
   For to bring my Mammie to,
In a hat with a long feather,
   And a trailing gown of blue;
And a company of fiddlers
   And a rout of maids and men
Danced the clock round to the morning,
   In a gay house-warming then.
And when all the guests were gone, and
   All was still as still can be,
In from the dark ivy hopped a
   Wee small bird: and that was Me.

Cake and Sack

Old King Caraway
  Supped on cake,
And a cup of sack
  His thirst to slake;
Bird in arras
  And hound in hall
Watched very softly
  Or not at all;
Fire in the middle,
  Stone all round
Changed not, heeded not,
  Made no sound;
All by himself
  At the Table High
He'd nibble and sip
  While his dreams slipped by;

And when he had finished,
  He'd nod and say,
'Cake and sack
  For King Caraway!'

The Ship of Rio

There was a ship of Rio
   Sailed out into the blue,
And nine and ninety monkeys
   Were all her jovial crew.
From bo'sun to the cabin boy,
   From quarter to caboose,
There weren't a stitch of calico
   To breech 'em—tight or loose;

28

From spar to deck, from deck to keel,
   From barnacle to shroud,
There weren't one pair of reach-me-downs
   To all that jabbering crowd.
But wasn't it a gladsome sight,
   When roared the deep sea gales,
To see them reef her fore and aft
   A-swinging by their tails!
Oh, wasn't it a gladsome sight,
When glassy calm did come,
To see them squatting tailor-wise
   Around a keg of rum!
Oh, wasn't it a gladsome sight,
   When in she sailed to land,
To see them all a-scampering skip
   For nuts across the sand!

Tillie

Old Tillie Turveycombe
Sat to sew,
Just where a patch of fern did grow;
There, as she yawned,
And yawn wide did she,
Floated some seed
Down her gull-e-t;
And look you once,
And look you twice,
Poor old Tillie
Was gone in a trice.
But oh, when the wind
Do a-moaning come,
'Tis poor old Tillie
Sick for home;
And oh, when a voice
In the mist do sigh,
Old Tillie Turveycombe's
Floating by.

Jim Jay

Do diddle di do,
  Poor Jim Jay
Got stuck fast
  In Yesterday.
Squinting he was,
  On cross-legs bent,
Never heeding
  The wind was spent.

Round veered the weathercock,
  The sun drew in——
And stuck was Jim
  Like a rusty pin. . . .
We pulled and we pulled
  From seven till twelve,
Jim, too frightened
  To help himself.
But all in vain.
  The clock struck one,
And there was Jim
  A little bit gone.
At half-past five
  You scarce could see
A glimpse of his flapping
  Handkerchee.
And when came noon,
  And we climbed sky-high,
Jim was a speck
Slip—slipping by.
Come to-morrow,
  The neighbours say,
He'll be past crying for;
  Poor Jim Jay.

Miss T.

It's a very odd thing——
  As odd as can be——
That whatever Miss T. eats
  Turns into Miss T.;
Porridge and apples,
  Mince, muffins and mutton,
Jam, junket, jumbles——
  Not a rap, not a button
It matters; the moment
  They're out of her plate,
Though shared by Miss Butcher
  And sour Mr. Bate;
Tiny and cheerful,
  And neat as can be,
Whatever Miss T. eats
  Turns into Miss T.

The Cupboard

I know a little cupboard,
With a teeny tiny key,
And there's a jar of Lollypops
    For me, me, me.

It has a little shelf, my dear,
As dark as dark can be,
And there's a dish of Banbury Cakes
    For me, me, me.

I have a small fat grandmamma,
With a very slippery knee,
And she's Keeper of the Cupboard,
    With the key, key, key.

And when I'm very good, my dear,
As good as good can be,
There's Banbury Cakes, and Lollypops
    For me, me, me.

Up and Down

Down the Hill of Ludgate,
    Up the Hill of Fleet,
To and fro and East and West
    With people flows the street;
Even the King of England
    On Temple Bar must beat
For leave to ride to Ludgate
    Down the Hill of Fleet.

The Barber's

Gold locks, and black locks
  Red locks, and brown,
Topknot to love-curl
  The hair wisps down;
Straight above the clear eyes,
  Rounded round the ears,
Snip-snap and snick-a-snick,
  Clash the Barber's shears;
Us, in the looking glass,
  Footsteps in the street,
Over, under, to and fro,
  The lean blades meet;
Bay Rum or Bear's Grease,
  A silver groat to pay——
Then out a-shin-shan-shining
  In the bright, blue day.

Hide and Seek

Hide and seek, says the Wind,
  In the shade of the woods;
Hide and seek, says the Moon,
  To the hazel buds;
Hide and seek, says the Cloud,
  Star on to star;
Hide and seek, says the Wave
  At the harbour bar;
Hide and seek, says I,
  To myself, and step
Out of the dream of Wake
  Into the dream of Sleep.

Mrs. Earth

Mrs. Earth makes silver black,
  Mrs. Earth makes iron red,
But Mrs. Earth can not stain gold
  Nor ruby red.
Mrs. Earth the slenderest bone
  Whitens in her bosom cold,
But Mrs. Earth can change my dreams
  No more than ruby or gold.
Mrs. Earth and Mr. Sun
  Can tan my skin, and tire my toes,
But all that I'm thinking of, ever shall think,
  Why, neither knows.

Then

Twenty, forty, sixty, eighty,
  A hundred years ago,
All through the night with lantern bright
  The Watch trudged to and fro.
And little boys tucked snug abed
  Would wake from dreams to hear——
'Two o' the morning by the clock,
  And the stars a-shining clear!'
Or, when across the chimney-tops
  Screamed shrill a North-East gale,
A faint and shaken voice would shout,
  'Three! and a storm of hail!'

The Window

Behind the blind I sit and watch
The people passing—passing by;
And not a single one can see
    My tiny watching eye.

They cannot see my little room,
All yellowed with the shaded sun,
They do not even know I'm here;
    Nor'll guess when I am gone.

Poor Henry

Thick in its glass
  The physic stands,
Poor Henry lifts
  Distracted hands;
His round cheek wans
  In the candlelight,
To smell that smell!
  To see that sight!

Finger and thumb
  Clinch his small nose,
A gurgle, a gasp,
  And down it goes;
Scowls Henry now;
  But mark that cheek,
Sleek with the bloom
  Of health next week!

Full Moon

One night as Dick lay fast asleep,
  Into his drowsy eyes
A great still light began to creep
  From out the silent skies.
It was the lovely moon's, for when
  He raised his dreamy head,
Her surge of silver filled the pane
  And streamed across his bed.
So, for awhile, each gazed at each——
  Dick and the solemn moon——
Till, climbing slowly on her way,
  She vanished, and was gone.

The Bookworm

'I'm tired—Oh, tired of books,' said Jack,
    'I long for meadows green,
And woods where shadowy violets
    Nod their cool leaves between;
I long to see the ploughman stride
    His darkening acres o'er,
To hear the hoarse sea-waters drive
    Their billows 'gainst the shore;
I long to watch the sea-mew wheel
    Back to her rock-perched mate;
Or, where the breathing cows are housed,
    Lean dreaming o'er the gate.
Something has gone, and ink and print
    Will never bring it back;
I long for the green fields again,
    I'm tired of books,' said Jack.

The Quartette

Tom sang for joy, and Ned sang for joy, and old Sam
    sang for joy;
All we four boys piped up loud, just like one boy;
And the ladies that sate with the Squire—their
    cheeks were all wet,
For the noise of the voice of us boys, when we sang
    our Quartette.

Tom he piped low and Ned he piped low and old
    Sam he piped low;
Into a sorrowful fall did our music flow;
And the ladies that sate with the Squire vowed
    they'd never forget,
How the eyes of them cried for delight, when we
    sang our Quartette.

Mistletoe

Sitting under the mistletoe
(Pale-green fairy mistletoe),
One last candle burning low,
All the sleepy dancers gone,
Just one candle burning on,
Shadows lurking everywhere:
Some one came, and kissed me there.

Tired I was; my head would go
Nodding under the mistletoe
(Pale-green, fairy mistletoe);
No footsteps came, no voice, but only,
Just as I sat there, sleepy, lonely,
Stooped in the still and shadowy air
Lips unseen—and kissed me there.

The Lost Shoe

Poor little Lucy
  By some mischance,
Lost her shoe
  As she did dance:
'Twas not on the stairs,
  Not in the hall;
Not where they sat
  At supper at all.
She looked in the garden,
  But there it was not;
Henhouse, or kennel,
  Or high dovecote.
Dairy and meadow,
  And wild woods through
Showed not a trace
  Of Lucy's shoe.
Bird nor bunny
  Nor glimmering moon
Breathed a whisper
  Of where 'twas gone.

It was cried and cried,
   Oyez and Oyez!
In French, Dutch, Latin
   And Portuguese.
Ships the dark seas
   Went plunging through,
But none brought news
   Of Lucy's shoe;
And still she patters
   In silk and leather,
O'er snow, sand, shingle,
   In every weather;
Spain, and Africa,
   Hindustan,
Java, China,
   And lamped Japan,
Plain and desert,
   She hops—hops through,
Pernambuco
   To gold Peru;
Mountain and forest,
   And river too,
All the world over
   For her lost shoe.

The Truants

Ere my heart beats too coldly and faintly
　To remember sad things, yet be gay,
I would sing a brief song of the world's little children
　Magic hath stolen away.

The primroses scattered by April,
　The stars of the wide Milky Way,
Cannot outnumber the hosts of the children
　Magic hath stolen away.

The buttercup green of the meadows,
　The snow of the blossoming may,
Lovelier are not than the legions of children
　Magic hath stolen away.

The waves tossing surf in the moonbeam,
　The Albatross lone on the spray,
Alone know the tears wept in vain for the children
　Magic hath stolen away.

In vain: for at hush of the evening,
　When the stars twinkle into the grey,
Seems to echo the far-away calling of children
　Magic hath stolen away.

Berries

There was an old woman
   Went blackberry picking
Along the hedges
   From Weep to Wicking.
Half a pottle——
   No more she had got,
When out steps a Fairy
   From her green grot;
And says, 'Well, Jill,
   Would 'ee pick 'ee mo?'
And Jill, she curtsys,
   And looks just so.
'Be off,' says the Fairy,
   'As quick as you can,

Over the meadows
  To the little green lane,
That dips to the hayfields
  Of Farmer Grimes:
I've berried those hedges
    A score of times;
Bushel on bushel
  I'll promise 'ee Jill,
This side of supper
  If 'ee pick with a will.'
She glints very bright,
  And speaks her fair;
Then lo, and behold!
  She had faded in air.

Be sure Old Goodie
  She trots betimes
Over the meadows
  To Farmer Grimes.
And never was queen
  With jewellery rich
As those same hedges
  From twig to ditch;
Like Dutchmen's coffers,
  Fruit, thorn, and flower——
They shone like William
  And Mary's bower.
And be sure Old Goodie
  Went back to Weep
So tired with her basket

She scarce could creep.
When she comes in the dusk
  To her cottage door,
There's Towser wagging
  As never before,
To see his Missus
  So glad to be
Come from her fruit-picking
  Back to—he.
As soon as next morning
  Dawn was grey,
The pot on the hob
  Was simmering away;
And all in a stew
  And a hugger-mugger
Towser and Jill
  A-boiling of sugar,
And the dark clear fruit
  That from Faërie came,
For syrup and jelly
  And blackberry jam.
Twelve jolly gallipots
  Jill put by;
And one little teeny one,
  One inch high;
And that she's hidden
  A good thumb deep,
Half-way over
  From Wicking to Weep.

Off the Ground

Three jolly Farmers
　　Once bet a pound
Each dance the others would
　　Off the ground.

Out of their coats
They slipped right soon,
And neat and nicesome,
Put each his shoon.

One—Two—three!——
And away they go,
Not too fast,
And not too slow;

Out from the elm-tree's
Noonday shadow,
Into the sun
And across the meadow.
Past the schoolroom,
With knees well bent
Fingers a-flicking,
They dancing went.
Up sides and over,
And round and round,
They crossed click-clacking,
The Parish bound.
By Tupman's meadow
They did their mile,
Tee-to-tum
On a three-barred stile.
Then straight through Whipham,
Downhill to Week,
Footing it lightsome,
But not too quick,
Up fields to Watchet,
And on through Wye,
Till seven fine churches
They'd seen skip by——
Seven fine churches,
And five old mills,
Farms in the valley,
And sheep on the hills;
Old Man's Acre
And Dead Man's Pool

All left behind,
As they danced through Wool.
And Wool gone by,
Like tops that seem
To spin in sleep
They danced in dream:
Withy—Wellover
Wassop—Wo——
Like an old clock
Their heels did go.
A league and a league
And a league they went,
And not one weary,
And not one spent.
And lo, and behold!
Past Willow-cum-Leigh
Stretched with its waters
The great green sea.

Says Farmer Bates,
'I puffs and I blows,
What's under the water,
Why, no man knows!'
Says Farmer Giles,
'My wind comes weak,
And a good man drownded
Is far to seek.'
But Farmer Turvey,
On twirling toes
Up's with his gaiters,

And in he goes:
Down where the mermaids
Pluck and play
On their twangling harps
In a sea-green day;
Down where the mermaids,
Finned and fair,
Sleek with their combs
Their yellow hair. . . .

Bates and Giles——
On the shingle sat,
Gazing at Turvey's
Floating hat.
But never a ripple
Nor bubble told
Where he was supping
Off plates of gold.
Never an echo
Rilled through the sea
Of the feasting and dancing
And minstrelsy.
They called—called—called:
Came no reply:
Naught but the ripples'
Sandy sigh.
Then glum and silent
They sat instead,
Vacantly brooding
On home and bed,

Till both together
Stood up and said:——
'Us knows not, dreams not,
Where you be,
Turvey, unless
In the deep blue sea;
But axcusing silver——
And it comes most willing——
Here's us two paying
Our forty shilling;
For it's sartin sure, Turvey,
Safe and sound,
You danced us square, Turvey;
Off the ground!'

The Thief at Robin's Castle

There came a Thief one night to Robin's Castle,
   He climbed up into a Tree;
And sitting with his head among the branches,
   A wondrous Sight did see.

For there was Robin supping at his table,
   With Candles of pure Wax,
His Dame and his two beauteous little Children,
   With Velvet on their backs.

Platters for each there were shin-shining,
   Of Silver many a pound,
And all of beaten Gold, three brimming Goblets,
   Standing the table round.

The smell that rose up richly from the Baked Meats
   Came thinning amid the boughs,
And much that greedy Thief who snuffed the night air—
   His Hunger did arouse.

He watched them eating, drinking, laughing, talking,
   Busy with finger and spoon,
While three most cunning Fiddlers, clad in crimson,
   Played them a supper-tune.

And he waited in the tree-top like a Starling,
   Till the Moon was gotten low;
When all the windows in the walls were darkened,
   He softly in did go.

There Robin and his Dame in bed were sleeping,
  And his Children young and fair;
Only Robin's Hounds from their warm kennels
  Yelped as he climbed the stair.

All, all were sleeping, page and fiddler,
  Cook, scullion, free from care;
Only Robin's Stallions from their stables
  Neighed as he climbed the stair.

A wee wan light the Moon did shed him,
  Hanging above the sea,
And he counted into his bag (of beaten Silver)
  Platters thirty-three.

Of Spoons three score; of jolly golden Goblets
  He stowed in four save one,
And six fine three-branched Cupid Candlesticks,
  Before his work was done.

Nine bulging bags of Money in a cupboard,
  Two snuffers, and a Dish
He found, the last all studded with great Garnets
  And shapen like a Fish.

Then tiptoe.up he stole into a Chamber,
  Where on Tasselled Pillows lay
Robin and his Dame in dreaming slumber,
  Tired with the summer's day.

That Thief he mimbled round him in the gloaming,
   Their Treasures for to spy,
Combs, Brooches, Chains, and Rings, and Pins
    and Buckles
   All higgledy piggle-dy.

A Watch shaped in the shape of a flat Apple
   In purest Crystal set,
He lifted from the hook where it was ticking
   And crammed in his Pochette.

He heaped the pretty Baubles on the table,
   Trinkets, Knick-knackerie,
Pearls, Diamonds, Sapphires, Topazes, and Opals——
   All in his bag put he.

And there in night's pale Gloom was Robin dreaming
   He was hunting the mountain Bear,
While his Dame in peaceful slumber in no wise heeded
   A greedy Thief was there.

And that ravenous Thief he climbed up even higher,
   Till into a chamber small
He crept where lay poor Robin's beauteous Children,
   Lovelier in sleep withal.

Oh, fairer was their Hair than Gold of Goblet,
   'Yond Silver their Cheeks did shine,
And their little hands that lay upon the linen
   Made that Thief's hard heart to pine.

But though a moment there his hard heart faltered,
  Eftsoons he took the twain,
And slipped them into his Bag with all his Plunder,
  And softly stole down again.

Spoon, Platter, Goblet, Ducats, Dishes, Trinkets,
  And those two Children dear,
A-quaking in the clinking and the clanking,
  And half bemused with fear.

He carried down the stairs into the Courtyard,
  But there he made no stay,
He just tied up his Garters, took a deep breath,
  And ran like the wind away.

Past Forest, River, Mountain, River, Forest——
  He coursed the whole night through,
Till morning found him come into a Country,
  Where none his bad face knew.

Past Mountain, River, Forest, River, Mountain——
  That Thief's lean shanks sped on,
Till Evening found him knocking at a Dark House,
  His breath now well-nigh gone.

There came a little maid and asked his Business;
  A Cobbler dwelt within;
And though she much misliked the Bag he carried,
  She led the Bad Man in.

He bargained with the Cobbler for a lodging
 And softly laid down his Sack——
In the Dead of Night, with none to spy or listen——
 From off his weary back.

And he taught the little Chicks to call him Father,
 And he sold his stolen Pelf,
And bought a Palace, Horses, Slaves, and Peacocks
 To ease his wicked self.

And though the Children never really loved him,
 He was rich past all belief;
While Robin and his Dame o'er Delf and Pewter
 Spent all their Days in Grief.

A Widow's Weeds

A poor old Widow in her weeds
Sowed her garden with wild-flower seeds;
Not too shallow, and not too deep,
And down came April—drip—drip—drip.
Up shone May, like gold, and soon
Green as an arbour grew leafy June.
And now all summer she sits and sews
Where willow herb, comfrey, and bugloss blows,
Teasle and tansy, meadowsweet,
Campion, toadflax, and rough hawksbit;
Brown bee orchis, and Peals of Bells;
Clover, burnet, and thyme she smells;
Like Oberon's meadows her garden is
Drowsy from dawn till dusk with bees.
Weeps she never, but sometimes sighs,
And peeps at her garden with bright brown eyes;
And all she has is all she needs——
A poor old Widow in her weeds.

'Sooeep!'

Black as a chimney is his face,
  And ivory white his teeth,
And in his brass-bound cart he rides,
  The chestnut blooms beneath.

'Sooeep, Sooeep!' he cries, and brightly peers
  This way and that, to see
With his two light-blue shining eyes
  What custom there may be.

And once inside the house, he'll squat,
  And drive his rods on high,
Till twirls his sudden sooty brush
  Against the morning sky.

Then 'mid his bulging bags of soot,
  With half the world asleep,
His small cart wheels him off again,
  Still hoarsely bawling, 'Sooeep!'

Mrs. MacQueen

With glass like a bull's-eye,
   And shutters of green,
Down on the cobbles
   Lives Mrs. MacQueen.

At six she rises;
   At nine you see
Her candle shine out
   In the linden tree:

And at half-past nine
   Not a sound is nigh,
But the bright moon's creeping
   Across the sky;

Or a far dog baying;
   Or a twittering bird
In its drowsy nest,
   In the darkness stirred;

Or like the roar
   Of a distant sea
A long-drawn *S-s-sh!*
   In the linden tree.

The Little Green Orchard

Some one is always sitting there,
        In the little green orchard;
  Even when the sun is high,
  In noon's unclouded sky,
  And faintly droning goes
  The bee from rose to rose,
  Some one in shadow is sitting there,
        In the little green orchard.

Yes, and when twilight's falling softly
        On the little green orchard;
  When the grey dew distils
  And every flower-cup fills;
  When the last blackbird says,
  'What—what!' and goes her way—ssh!
I have heard voices calling softly
        In the little green orchard.

Not that I am afraid of being there,
            In the little green orchard;
    Why, when the moon's been bright,
    Shedding her lonesome light,
    And moths like ghosties come,
    And the horned snail leaves home:
I've sat there, whispering and listening there,
            In the little green orchard;

Only it's strange to be feeling there,
            In the little green orchard,
    Whether you paint or draw,
    Dig, hammer, chop, or saw;
    When you are most alone,
    All but the silence gone . . .
Some one is waiting and watching there,
            In the little green orchard.

Poor 'Miss 7'

Lone and alone she lies
   Poor Miss 7,
Five steep flights from the earth,
   And one from heaven;
Dark hair and dark brown eyes,——
Not to be sad she tries,
Still—still it's lonely lies
   Poor Miss 7.

One day-long watch hath she,
  Poor Miss 7,
Not in some orchard sweet
  In April Devon,——
Just four blank walls to see,
And dark come shadowily,
No moon, no stars, ah me!
  Poor Miss 7.

And then to wake again,
  Poor Miss 7,
To the cold night, to have
  Sour physic given;
Out of some dream of pain,
Then strive long hours in vain
Deep dreamless sleep to gain:
  Poor Miss 7.

Yet memory softly sings
  Poor Miss 7,
Songs full of love and peace
  And gladness even;
Clear flowers and tiny wings,
All tender, lovely things,
Hope to her bosom brings——
  Happy Miss 7.

Sam

When Sam goes back in memory,
   It is to where the sea
Breaks on the shingle, emerald-green,
   In white foam, endlessly;
He says—with small brown eye on mine—
   'I used to keep awake,
And lean from my window in the moon,
   Watching those billows break.
And half a million tiny hands,
   And eyes, like sparks of frost,
Would dance and come tumbling into the moon,
   On every breaker tossed.

And all across from star to star,
　　I've seen the watery sea,
With not a single ship in sight,
　　Just ocean there, and me;
And heard my father snore. And once,
　　As sure as I'm alive,
Out of those wallowing, moon-flecked waves
　　I saw a mermaid dive;
Head and shoulders above the wave,
　　Plain as I now see you,
Combing her hair, now back, now front,
　　Her two eyes peeping through;
Calling me, "Sam!"—quietlike—"Sam!" . . .
　　But me . . . I never went,
Making believe I kind of thought
　　'Twas some one else she meant . . .
Wonderful lovely there she sat,
　　Singing the night away,
All in the solitudinous sea
　　Of that there lonely bay.
P'raps,' and he'd smooth his hairless mouth,
　　'P'raps, if 'twere now, my son,
P'raps, if I heard a voice say, "Sam!" . . .
　　Morning would find me gone.'

Andy Battle

Once and there was a young sailor, yeo ho!
  And he sailed out over the say
For the isles where pink coral and palm branches
                                              blow.
  And the fire-flies turn night into day,
                              Yeo ho!
And the fire-flies turn night into day.

But the *Dolphin* went down in a tempest, yeo ho!
  And with three forsook sailors ashore,
The *Portingales* took him where sugar-canes grow,
  Their slave for to be evermore,
                              Yeo ho!
Their slave for to be evermore.

With his musket for mother and brother, yeo ho!
  He warred with the Cannibals drear,
In forests where panthers pad soft to and fro,
  And the *Pongo* shakes noonday with fear,
                              Yeo ho!
And the *Pongo* shakes noonday with fear.

Now lean with long travail, all wasted with woe,
  With a monkey for messmate and friend,
He sits 'neath the *Cross* in the cankering snow,
  And waits for his sorrowful end,
                              Yeo ho!
And waits for his sorrowful end.

The Old Soldier

There came an Old Soldier to my door,
Asked a crust, and asked no more;
The wars had thinned him very bare,
Fighting and marching everywhere,
  With a Fol rol dol rol di do.

With nose stuck out, and cheek sunk in,
A bristling beard upon his chin——
Powder and bullets and wounds and drums
Had come to that Soldier as suchlike comes——
  With a Fol rol dol rol di do.

'Twas sweet and fresh with buds of May,
Flowers springing from every spray;
And when he had supped the Old Soldier trolled
The song of youth that never grows old,
   Called Fol rol dol rol di do.

Most of him rags, and all of him lean,
And the belt round his belly drawn tightsome in,
He lifted his peaked old grizzled head,
And these were the very same words he said——
   A Fol-rol-dol-rol-*di*-do.

The Picture

Here is a sea-legged sailor,
  Come to this tottering Inn,
Just when the bronze on its signboard is fading,
  And the black shades of evening begin.

With his head on thick paws sleeps a sheepdog,
  There stoops the Shepherd, and see,
All follow-my-leader the ducks waddle homeward,
    Under the sycamore tree.

Very brown is the face of the Sailor,
  His bundle is crimson, and green
Are the thick leafy boughs that hang dense o'er
        the Tavern,
  And blue the far meadows between.

But the Crust, Ale and Cheese of the Sailor,
  His Mug and his platter of Delf,
And the crescent to light home the Shepherd
        and Sheepdog
  The painter has kept to himself.

The Little Old Cupid

'Twas a very small garden;
  The paths were of stone,
Scattered with leaves,
  With moss overgrown;
And a little old Cupid
  Stood under a tree,
With a small broken bow
  He stood aiming at me.

The dog-rose in briars
  Hung over the weeds,
The air was aflock
  With the floating of seeds;

And a little old Cupid
   Stood under a tree,
With a small broken bow
   He stood aiming at me.

The dovecote was tumbling,
   The fountain dry,
A wind in the orchard
   Went whispering by;
And a little old Cupid
   Stood under a tree,
With a small broken bow
   He stood aiming at me.

King David

King David was a sorrowful man:
    No cause for his sorrow had he:
And he called for the music of a hundred harps,
    To ease his melancholy.

They played till they all fell silent:
    Played—and play sweet did they;
But the sorrow that haunted the heart of King David
    They could not charm away.

He rose; and in his garden
    Walked by the moon alone,
A nightingale hidden in a cypress-tree
    Jargoned on and on.

King David lifted his sad eyes
    Into the dark-boughed tree——
'Tell me, thou little bird that singest,
    Who taught my grief to thee?'

But the bird in no wise heeded;
    And the king in the cool of the moon
Hearkened to the nightingale's sorrowfulness,
    Till all his own was gone.

The Old House

A very, very old house I know——
And ever so many people go,
Past the small lodge, forlorn and still,
Under the heavy branches, till
Comes the blank wall, and there's the door.
Go in they do; come out no more.
No voice says aught; no spark of light
Across that threshold cheers the sight;
Only the evening star on high
Less lonely makes a lonely sky,
As, one by one, the people go
Into that very old house I know.

Unstooping

Low on his fours the Lion
    Treads with the surly Bear;
But Men straight upward from the dust
   Walk with their heads in air;
The free sweet winds of heaven,
   The sunlight from on high
  Beat on their clear bright cheeks and brows
   As they go striding by;
The doors of all their houses
   They arch so they may go,
Uplifted o'er the four-foot beasts,
   Unstooping, to and fro.

All But Blind

All but blind
  In his chambered hole
Gropes for worms
  The four-clawed Mole.

All but blind
  In the evening sky
The hooded Bat
  Twirls softly by.

All but blind
  In the burning day
The Barn Owl blunders
  On her way.

And blind as are
  These three to me,
So, blind to Some One
  I must be.

Nicholas Nye

Thistle and darnel and dock grew there,
  And a bush, in the corner, of may,
On the orchard wall I used to sprawl
  In the blazing heat of the day;
Half asleep and half awake,
  While the birds went twittering by,
And nobody there my lone to share
    But Nicholas Nye.

Nicholas Nye was lean and grey,
  Lame of a leg and old,
More than a score of donkey's years
  He had seen since he was foaled;
He munched the thistles, purple and **spiked**,
  Would sometimes stoop and sigh,
And turn his head, as if he said,
    'Poor Nicholas Nye!'

Alone with his shadow he'd drowse in the meadow,
  Lazily swinging his tail,
At break of day he used to bray,——
  Not much too hearty and hale;
But a wonderful gumption was under his skin,
  And a clear calm light in his eye,
And once in a while—he'd smile . . .
    Would Nicholas Nye.

Seem to be smiling at me, he would,
  From his bush in the corner, of may,——
Bony and ownerless, widowed and worn,
  Knobble-kneed, lonely and grey;
And over the grass would seem to pass
  'Neath the deep dark blue of the sky,
Something much better than words between me
    And Nicholas Nye.

But dusk would come in the apple boughs,
  The green of the glow-worm shine,
The birds in nest would crouch to rest,
  And home I'd trudge to mine;
And there, in the moonlight, dark with dew,
  Asking not wherefore nor why,
Would brood like a ghost, and as still as a post,
    Old Nicholas Nye.

The Pigs
and the Charcoal-Burner

The old Pig said to the little pigs,
  'In the forest is truffles and mast,
Follow me then, all ye little pigs,
    Follow me fast!'

The Charcoal-burner sat in the shade
  With his chin on his thumb,
And saw the big Pig and the little pigs,
    Chuffling come.

He watched 'neath a green and giant bough,
  And the pigs in the ground
Made a wonderful grizzling and gruzzling
    And a greedy sound.

And when, full-fed, they were gone, and Night
  Walked her starry ways,
He stared with his cheeks in his hands
    At his sullen blaze.

Five Eyes

In Hans' old Mill his three black cats
Watch the bins for the thieving rats.
Whisker and claw, they crouch in the night,
Their five eyes smouldering green and bright:
Squeaks from the flour sacks, squeaks from where
The cold wind stirs on the empty stair,
Squeaking and scampering, everywhere.
Then down they pounce, now in, now out,
At whisking tail, and sniffing snout;
While lean old Hans he snores away
Till peep of light at break of day;
Then up he climbs to his creaking mill,
Out come his cats all grey with meal——
Jekkel, and Jessup, and one-eyed Jill.

Tit for Tat

Have you been catching of fish, Tom Noddy?
  Have you snared a weeping hare?
Have you whistled, 'No Nunny,' and gunned a poor
    bunny,
  Or a blinded bird of the air?

Have you trod like a murderer through the green
    woods,
  Through the dewy deep dingles and glooms,
While every small creature screamed shrill to Dame
    Nature,
  'He comes—and he comes!'?

Wonder I very much do, Tom Noddy,
  If ever, when you are a-roam,
An Ogre from space will stoop a lean face
  And lug you home:

Lug you home over his fence, Tom Noddy,
  Of thorn-sticks nine yards high,
With your bent knees strung round his old iron gun
  And your head dan-dangling by:

And hang you up stiff on a hook, Tom Noddy,
  From a stone-cold pantry shelf,
Whence your eyes will glare in an empty stare,
  Till you're cooked yourself!

Earth Folk

The cat she walks on padded claws,
The wolf on the hills lays stealthy paws,
Feathered birds in the rain-sweet sky
At their ease in the air, flit low, flit high.

The oak's blind, tender roots pierce deep,
His green crest towers, dimmed in sleep,
Under the stars whose thrones are set
Where never prince hath journeyed yet.

Grim

Beside the blaze of forty fires
   Giant Grim doth sit,
Roasting a thick-woolled mountain sheep
   Upon an iron spit.
Above him wheels the winter sky,
   Beneath him, fathoms deep,
Lies hidden in the valley mists
   A village fast asleep——
Save for one restive hungry dog
   That, snuffing towards the height,
Smells Grim's broiled supper-meat, and spies
   His watch-fire twinkling bright.

Summer Evening

The sandy cat by the Farmer's chair
Mews at his knee for dainty fare;
Old Rover in his moss-greened house
Mumbles a bone, and barks at a mouse;
In the dewy fields the cattle lie
Chewing the cud 'neath a fading sky;
Dobbin at manger pulls his hay:
Gone is another summer's day.

At the Keyhole

'Grill me some bones,' said the Cobbler,
  'Some bones, my pretty Sue;
I'm tired of my lonesome with heels and soles,
Springsides and uppers too;
A mouse in the wainscot is nibbling;
A wind in the keyhole drones;
And a sheet webbed over my candle, Susie,——
  Grill me some bones!'

'Grill me some bones,' said the Cobbler,
  'I sat at my tic-tac-to;
And a footstep came to my door and stopped,
And a hand groped to and fro;
And I peered up over my boot and last;
And my feet went cold as stones:——
I saw an eye at the keyhole, Susie!——
  Grill me some bones!'

The Old Stone House

Nothing on the grey roof, nothing on the brown,
Only a little greening where the rain drips down;
Nobody at the window, nobody at the door,
Only a little hollow which a foot once wore;
But still I tread on tiptoe, still tiptoe on I go,
Past nettles, porch, and weedy well, for oh, I know
A friendless face is peering, and a still clear eye
Peeps closely through the casement as my step goes by.

The Ruin

When the last colours of the day
Have from their burning ebbed away,
About that ruin, cold and lone,
The cricket shrills from stone to stone;
And scattering o'er its darkened green,
Bands of the fairies may be seen,
Chattering like grasshoppers, their feet
Dancing a thistledown dance round it:
While the great gold of the mild moon
Tinges their tiny acorn shoon.

The Ride-By-Nights

Up on their brooms the Witches stream,
Crooked and black in the crescent's gleam;
One foot high, and one foot low,
Bearded, cloaked, and cowled, they go,
'Neath Charlie's Wain they twitter and tweet,
And away they swarm 'neath the Dragon's feet,
With a whoop and a flutter they swing and sway,
And surge pell-mell down the Milky Way.
Betwixt the legs of the glittering Chair
They hover and squeak in the empty air.
Then round they swoop past the glimmering Lion
To where Sirius barks behind huge Orion;
Up, then, and over to wheel amain,
Under the silver, and home again.

Peak and Puke

From his cradle in the glamourie
They have stolen my wee brother,
Housed a changeling in his swaddlings
For to fret my own poor mother.
Pules it in the candle light
Wi' a cheek so lean and white,
Chinkling up its eyne so wee
Wailing shrill at her an' me.
It we'll neither rock nor tend
Till the Silent Silent send,
Lapping in their waesome arms
Him they stole with spells and charms,
Till they take this changeling creature
Back to its own fairy nature——
Cry! Cry! as long as may be,
Ye shall ne'er be woman's baby!

The Changeling

'Ahoy, and ahoy!'
  'Twixt mocking and merry——
'Ahoy and ahoy, there,
  Young man of the ferry!'

She stood on the steps
  In the watery gloom——
That Changeling—'Ahoy, there!'
  She called him to come.
He came on the green wave,
  He came on the grey,
Where stooped that sweet lady
  That still summer's day.
He fell in a dream
  Of her beautiful face,
As she sat on the thwart
  And smiled in her place.

No echo his oar woke,
  Float silent did they,
Past low-grazing cattle
  In the sweet of the hay.
And still in a dream
  At her beauty sat he,
Drifting stern foremost
  Down—down to the sea.

Come you, then: call,
  When the twilight apace
Brings shadow to brood
  On the loveliest face;
You shall hear o'er the water
  Ring faint in the grey——
'Ahoy, and ahoy, there!'
  And tremble away;
'Ahoy, and ahoy! . . .'
  And tremble away.

The Mocking Fairy

'Won't you look out of your window, Mrs. Gill?'
  Quoth the Fairy, nidding, nodding in the garden;
'*Can't* you look out of your window, Mrs. Gill?'
  Quoth the Fairy, laughing softly in the garden;
But the air was still, the cherry boughs were still,
And the ivy-tod neath the empty sill,
And never from her window looked out Mrs. Gill
  On the Fairy shrilly mocking in the garden.

'What have they done with you, you poor Mrs. Gill?'
  Quoth the Fairy brightly glancing in the garden;
'Where have they hidden you, you poor old Mrs. Gill?'
  Quoth the Fairy dancing lightly in the garden;

But night's faint veil now wrapped the hill,
Stark 'neath the stars stood the dead-still Mill,
And out of her cold cottage never answered Mrs. Gill
  The Fairy mimbling, mambling in the garden.

The Honey Robbers

There were two Fairies, Gimmul and Mel,
Loved Earth Man's honey passing well;
Oft at the hives of his tame bees
They would their sugary thirst appease.

When dusk began to darken to night,
They would hie along in the fading light,
With elf-locked hair and scarlet lips,
And small stone knives to slit the skeps,
So softly not a bee inside
Should hear the woven straw divide:
And then with sly and greedy thumbs
Would rifle the sweet honeycombs.

And drowsily drone to drone would say,
'A cold, cold wind blows in this way';
And the great Queen would turn her head
From face to face, astonishèd,
And, though her maids with comb and brush
Would comb and soothe and whisper, 'Hush!'
About the hive would shrilly go
A keening—keening, to and fro;
At which those robbers 'neath the trees
Would taunt and mock the honey-bees,
And through their sticky teeth would buzz
Just as an angry hornet does.

And when this Gimmul and this Mel
Had munched and sucked and swilled their fill,
Or ever Man's first cock could crow
Back to their Faërie Mounds they'd go;
Edging across the twilight air,
Thieves of a guise remotely fair.

Longlegs

Longlegs—he yelled 'Coo-ee!'
   And all across the combe
Shrill and shrill it rang—rang through
   The clear green gloom.
Fairies there were a-spinning,
   And a white tree-maid
Lifted her eyes, and listened
   In her rain-sweet glade.
Bunnie to bunnie stamped; old Wat
   Chin-deep in bracken sate;
A throstle piped, 'I'm by, I'm by!'
   Clear to his timid mate.
And there was Longlegs straddling,
   And hearkening was he,
To distant Echo thrilling back
   A thin 'Coo-ee!'

Bewitched

I have heard a lady this night,
  Lissom and jimp and slim,
Calling me—calling me over the heather,
  'Neath the beech boughs dusk and dim.

I have followed a lady this night,
  Followed her far and lone,
Fox and adder and weasel know
  The ways that we have gone.

I sit at my supper 'mid honest faces,
  And crumble my crust and say
Naught in the long-drawn drawl of the voices
  Talking the hours away.

I'll go to my chamber under the gable,
  And the moon will lift her light
In at my lattice from over the moorland
  Hollow and still and bright.

And I know she will shine on a lady of witchcraft,
  Gladness and grief to see,
Who has taken my heart with her nimble fingers,
  Calls in my dreams to me;

Who has led me a dance by dell and dingle
  My human soul to win,
Made me a changeling to my own, own mother,
  A stranger to my kin.

Melmillo

Three and thirty birds there stood
In an elder in a wood;
Called Melmillo—flew off three,
Leaving thirty in the tree;
Called Melmillo—nine now gone,
And the boughs held twenty-one;
Called Melmillo—and eighteen
Left but three to nod and preen;
Called Melmillo—three—two—one
Now of birds were feathers none.

Then stole slim Melmillo in
To that wood all dusk and green,
And with lean long palms outspread
Softly a strange dance did tread;

Not a note of music she
Had for echoing company;
All the birds were flown to rest
In the hollow of her breast;
In the wood—thorn, elder, willow——
Danced alone—lone danced Melmillo.

Trees

Of all the trees in England,
  Her sweet three corners in,
Only the Ash, the bonnie Ash
  Burns fierce while it is green.

Of all the trees in England,
  From sea to sea again,
The Willow loveliest stoops her boughs
  Beneath the driving rain.

Of all the trees in England,
  Past frankincense and myrrh,
There's none for smell, of bloom or smoke,
  Like Lime and Juniper.

Of all the trees in England,
  Oak, Elder, Elm and Thorn,
The Yew alone burns lamps of peace
  For them that lie forlorn.

Silver

Slowly, silently, now the moon
Walks the night in her silver shoon;
This way, and that, she peers, and sees
Silver fruit upon silver trees;
One by one the casements catch
Her beams beneath the silvery thatch;
Couched in his kennel, like a log,
With paws of silver sleeps the dog;
From their shadowy cote the white breasts peep
Of doves in a silver-feathered sleep;
A harvest mouse goes scampering by,
With silver claws, and silver eye;
And moveless fish in the water gleam,
By silver reeds in a silver stream.

Nobody Knows

Often I've heard the Wind sigh
  By the ivied orchard wall,
Over the leaves in the dark night,
  Breathe a sighing call,
And faint away in the silence,
  While I, in my bed,
Wondered, 'twixt dreaming and waking,
    What it said.

Nobody knows what the Wind is,
  Under the height of the sky,
Where the hosts of the stars keep far away house
  And its wave sweeps by——
Just a great wave of the air,
  Tossing the leaves in its sea,
And foaming under the eaves of the roof
    That covers me.

And so we live under deep water,
  All of us, beasts and men,
And our bodies are buried down under the sand,
  When we go again;
And leave, like the fishes, our shells,
  And float on the Wind and away,
To where, o'er the marvellous tides of the air,
  Burns day.

Will Ever?

Will he ever be weary of wandering,
   The flaming sun?
Ever weary of waning in lovelight,
   The white still moon?
Will ever a shepherd come
   With a crook of simple gold,
And lead all the little stars
   Like lambs to the fold?

Will ever the Wanderer sail
   From over the sea,
Up the river of water,
   To the stones to me?
Will he take us all into his ship,
   Dreaming, and waft us far,
To where in the clouds of the West
   The Islands are?

Many a Mickle

A little sound——
Only a little, a little——
The breath in a reed,
A trembling fiddle;
A trumpet's ring,
The shuddering drum;
So all the glory, bravery, hush
Of music come.

A little sound——
Only a stir and a sigh
Of each green leaf
Its fluttering neighbour by;
Oak on to oak,
The wide dark forest through——
So o'er the watery wheeling world
The night winds go.

A little sound,
Only a little, a little——
The thin high drone
Of the simmering kettle,
The gathering frost,
The click of needle and thread;
Mother, the fading wall, the dream,
The drowsy bed.

Wanderers

Wide are the meadows of night
And daisies are shining there,
Tossing their lovely dews,
Lustrous and fair;
And through these sweet fields go,
Wanderers 'mid the stars——
Venus, Mercury, Uranus, Neptune,
Saturn, Jupiter, Mars.

'Tired in their silver, they move,
And circling, whisper and say,
Fair are the blossoming meads of delight
Through which we stray.

The Song of the Secret

Where is beauty?
   Gone, gone:
The cold winds have taken it
   With their faint moan;
The white stars have shaken it,
   Trembling down,
Into the pathless deeps of the sea:
   Gone, gone
   Is beauty from me.

The clear naked flower
   Is faded and dead;
The green-leafed willow,
   Drooping her head,
Whispers low to the shade
   Of her boughs in the stream;
   Sighing a beauty
   Secret as dream.

111

The Song of the Soldiers

As I sat musing by the frozen dyke,
There was one man marching with a bright steel pike,
Marching in the dayshine like a ghost came he,
And behind me was the moaning and the murmur of
    the sea.

As I sat musing, 'twas not one but ten——
Rank on rank of ghostly soldiers marching o'er the fen,
Marching in the misty air they showed in dreams to me,
And behind me was the shouting and the shattering of
    the sea.

As I sat musing, 'twas a host in dark array,
With their horses and their cannon wheeling onward to
    the fray,
Moving like a shadow to the fate the brave must dree,
And behind me roared the drums, rang the trumpets of
    the sea.

The Bees' Song

Thousandz of thornz there be
On the Rozez where gozez
The Zebra of Zee:
Sleek, striped, and hairy,
The steed of the Fairy
Princess of Zee.

Heavy with blossomz be
The Rozez that growzez
In the thickets of Zee.
Where grazez the Zebra,
Marked Abracadeeebra,
Of the Princess of Zee.

And he nozez the poziez
Of the Rozez that growzez
So luvez'm and free,
With an eye, dark and wary,
In search of a Fairy,
Whose Rozez he knowzez
Were not honeyed for he,
But to breathe a sweet incense
To solace the Princess
Of far-away Zee.

Song of Enchantment

A Song of Enchantment I sang me there,
In a green—green wood, by waters fair,
Just as the words came up to me
I sang it under the wildwood tree.

Widdershins turned I, singing it low,
Watching the wild birds come and go;
No cloud in the deep dark blue to be seen
Under the thick-thatched branches green.

Twilight came; silence came;
The planet of Evening's silver flame;
By darkening paths I wandered through
Thickets trembling with drops of dew.

But the music is lost and the words are gone
Of the song I sang as I sat alone,
Ages and ages have fallen on me——
On the wood and the pool and the elder tree.

Dream-Song

Sunlight, moonlight,
   Twilight, starlight——
Gloaming at the close of day,
   And an owl calling,
   Cool dews falling
In a wood of oak and may.

   Lantern-light, taper-light,
   Torchlight, no-light:
Darkness at the shut of day,
   And lions roaring,
   Their wrath pouring
In wild waste places far away.

   Elf-light, bat-light,
   Touchwood-light and toad-light,
And the sea a shimmering gloom of grey,
   And a small face smiling
   In a dream's beguiling
In a world of wonders far away.

The Song of the Shadows

Sweep thy faint strings, Musician,
    With thy long lean hand;
Downward the starry tapers burn,
    Sinks soft the waning sand;
The old hound whimpers couched in sleep,
    The embers smoulder low;
Across the walls the shadows
        Come, and go.

Sweep softly thy strings, Musician,
    The minutes mount to hours;
Frost on the windless casement weaves
    A labyrinth of flowers;
Ghosts linger in the darkening air,
    Hearken at the open door;
Music hath called them, dreaming,
        Home once more.

The Song of the Mad Prince

Who said, 'Peacock Pie'?
  The old King to the sparrow:
Who said, 'Crops are ripe'?
  Rust to the harrow:
Who said, 'Where sleeps she now?
  Where rests she now her head,
Bathed in eve's loveliness'?——
  That's what I said.

Who said, 'Ay, mum's the word'?
  Sexton to willow:
Who said, 'Green dusk for dreams,
  Moss for a pillow'?

Who said, 'All Time's delight
  Hath she for narrow bed;
Life's troubled bubble broken'?——
  That's what I said.

The Song of 'Finis'

At the edge of All the Ages
   A Knight sate on his steed,
His armour red and thin with rust,
   His soul from sorrow freed;
And he lifted up his visor
   From a face of skin and bone,
And his horse turned head and whinnied
   As the twain stood there alone.

No Bird above that steep of time
  Sang of a livelong quest;
No wind breathed,
      Rest:
'Lone for an end!' cried Knight to steed,
  Loosed an eager rein——
Charged with his challenge into Space:
  And quiet did quiet remain.